30 Days to Prosperity

A Workbook to Manifest Abundance

GAIL THACKRAY

Printed in the United States of America

Thackray, Gail

30 Days to Prosperity A Workbook to Manifest Abundance/by Gail Thackray

ISBN-13: 978-0-9848440-0-5

Project and Developmental Editor, Mara Krausz
Cover and interior design by Teagarden Designs
Author photograph by Kevin Ellsworth
Copy editing by Kathy Glass

Published by
Indian Springs Publishing
P.O. Box 286
La Cañada, CA 91012
www.indianspringspublishing.com

The power is within you to create all that you desire, all you have to do is ask.

TABLE OF CONTENTS

SECTION ONE

SECTION TWO

SECTION ONE

Introduction

I am one of those people who have gone from the top of the financial game to the bottom and back again on more than one occasion. Perhaps I take more risks than most. I have gone from owning and running multi-million dollar companies, not worrying about money, to being worried about making ends meet and whether the electricity would be cut off. Then, somehow I manage to recover and get back up again. It's that "somehow" that we are going to talk about in this book.

It was during my worst financial slump that I really started digging for solutions and asking the question "Why am I experiencing this?" and pleading, "Please God, I have learned my lesson. Let me get back to where I was and this time I promise to be more responsible."

I searched the subjects of business, money, the psyche, and energy associated with success. There are many books, tapes, and manuals on these subjects, but I couldn't find a practical guide that worked for me. I found books that were interesting and had really good advice, but once I put the book down, life's worries would catch back up with me. The lessons I had learned would go by the wayside. I wouldn't apply any of the knowledge in my life. I needed to write, for myself, a practical program that I would follow and that would change my life permanently.

I have been psychically intuitive from a young age, but at age forty I had a life-changing experience through which I realized that I am, in fact, a medium able to receive messages from people who have passed over.

I continued working in my mundane businesses as I pursued this newly found talent. At first I just practiced on friends and passed on messages from spirit. Pretty soon I was being asked to lecture and teach, and was overbooked with professional readings.

Things that I had once thought were entirely my creation or my thoughts, I now believe are often guidance from the other side. I believe strongly that we all have a "team" or a guidance system that follows us through life and directs us. In fact, your spirit guides may have played a part in your reading this book.

As I opened up to this "other world," it was as if it had always been there, always working with me, I just hadn't paid attention. I've learned to consider this awareness not as a special talent of mine, but rather as a connection that we all have, with the potential of receiving help from these other energies around us. We are all part of it, we are all connected; it's just that most of us are too busy with our physical lives to live and feel the connection to our spiritual life.

My sideline work soon progressed into teaching and helping others communicate with the other side to receive Divine guidance and assistance in their lives. My "psychic" abilities to talk to spirits, communicate with animals, help others heal, or to manifest things in my own life were not "psychic" talents. In fact, they were not talents at all but rather I had finally discovered a clearer connection to Divine Source or God. I had developed a connection to my subconscious, to those energies unseen and to our collective consciousness. In doing so, I had opened up many abilities or tools that I now have access to.

Even with the knowledge that we are all connected and an understanding of a higher power that we are able to tap into, many of us still don't have the "tools" to specifically apply this in our daily lives. I had finally found these tools and was learning to tap in and to help others do the same.

It was right about the time that my business and financial life hit rock bottom that I discovered this other power beyond my physical realm and how to tap into it, not only to turn my life around but to give me the financial freedom I had been seeking.

I had given up on the fight to hold on to my credit. With my debts out of control and the economy starting in a downward spiral, my regular businesses were failing drastically and vendors were not paying. I had hit rock bottom. As I asked for answers to my financial situation, I started to look to my guides. I was given insights and I began to write them down. This was a guide that I was writing for myself. I needed all the advice I had ever read or learned before, but I needed it in an easy format that I could follow and stick to.

I realized that there is a strong connection between our subconscious—what we think and say—and what appears in our life. I started to formulate these ideas into an actual program that I could commit to following. Immediately I saw an improvement in my financial situation. Checks started to come in from unexpected sources. I would receive cash amounts in odd ways from projects that I had forgotten about. Doors seemed to open up and direct me. New business opportunities started to be offered, and financial freedom was well on its way.

Through my psychic readings, I was coaching more and more people who had the same financial worries as I did. Wanting to provide more help to my clients, I felt the urge to write this book and explain these methods to others. In fact, I felt like I was being nudged from the "other side" to get down and write. This book is not "channeled" from the other side *per se*, although I can't completely decipher what is my own advice, my own experience and thoughts, and what is the spiritual direction that I am clearly receiving. But it is a mixture of the practical business side of me and the spirit helpers who work through me, whom I have come to love and accept as part of me.

Although I am a medium and psychic, I am also one who finds it very hard to believe in anything that is not physically there or cannot be proven scientifically.

I am not your stereotypical New Age type. I excelled in science and math as a student. I went on to create, own, and manage successful corporations and worked as a business consultant for some very notable organizations. In fact, I was quite entrenched in the whole rat race and very much part of the corporate battleground. I just happened to have found my psychic side, too.

Don't be put off if you don't believe in the spiritual realm or New Age thought. If you follow this workbook, it will work. If you are religious and want to consider this work through prayer and asking God for guidance, that is fine. Just replace the word "meditation" with "prayer" and the words "Divine Source Energy" with "God." It doesn't matter how you approach it. It is not necessary to know the how or why it works. It does work!

How To Use This Book

This book is divided into two sections. Section I explains how and why this program works, discusses what your subconscious really is, and describes the energy of money and why we attract or reject better financial situations. Section II is the 30-day workbook of exercises to program your subconscious.

It is preferable that you read Section I initially. However, this program will work regardless. If you want to jump right in, you can start your 30-day program while you are still reading Section I. Even if you don't believe, fully grasp, or understand the underlying concepts, your 30-day program will still be successful. You do not need to be consciously aware of how or why it works.

Part of your work will include programming a pendant, piece of jewelry, stone, or other type of trinket that you will use as a tool to aid you in concentrating your energy into your subconscious and enabling its programming as you work through this 30-day program.

If you diligently follow this workbook of daily exercises, your subconscious will be programmed to bring you the means and the ability to manifest the abundance you desire.

Money, An Energy Source

Why is it that some people can earn millions, end up in bankruptcy, and then start all over gaining back their millions again, while others struggle just to keep the status quo? Is it that some are just lucky? Is it that some are better educated? What is it that makes some of us rich and some of us poor? Is it that we all have a financial blueprint and some have a blueprint to be rich and some to be poor, and if so, can we change that blueprint?

Money is a subject that stirs great feeling in all of us. Its uses can give us great happiness and joy, yet the lack of it can create feelings of fear, depression, and worthlessness.

Money itself has no energy. It is a piece of paper or a piece of metal, but it is the energy behind money that creates so much happiness and so much sorrow. So why is it that some people are blessed to receive all that they need and want, and others are not? And some have much more than they need and are still not happy. It is all based on the energy of money and how each of us perceives and uses that energy.

To say that money is not important or money doesn't buy happiness is to be naive. Yes, money alone cannot buy true happiness, but in this world money can give us the freedom to live our lives as we please. It can give us security and tranquility of mind. It can provide us with experiences that we may not otherwise be able to have. Money is one of the energies through which we experience life with ease or with strife.

The feelings of guilt, greed, and competition that often come with the striving for money are simply an attachment to the physical money itself and a misplaced interpretation or use of the energy. A desire for money for money's sake, rather than for the good that it can bring forth, is an unhealthy attachment that can bring you lack and unhappiness.

We were all born to be rich. There is an endless supply of money that we can all create and manifest in our lives if we learn to act and think in a way that vibrates with our natural ability to attract all that we desire.

We need to stop attaching ourselves to physical money and our physical sources of income and start relying on our inner selves, our subconscious, which is the real source of all the abundance we will ever need and desire. When we are aligned correctly and our subconscious is working for us, we need only think of our desires, and the money or the means that is needed to fulfill these desires will flow to us.

Our subconscious works automatically, all the time, in the same way that our heart pumps blood and our lungs breathe for us. Our subconscious brings to us what we desire. The issue here is learning to program our subconscious to bring us things that we desire and to stop things appearing in our life that we do not desire. In particular, how do we program our subconscious to deliver us the means or the financial resources for all that we desire?

Money is made up of two energies: how we use our money physically and rationally, such as how we budget and save, invest and spend, and maintain our awareness of money on a conscious level; and second, the subconscious energy of money, which is driven by our thoughts and emotions.

Currently, we are in an economic slump with the stock market falling daily, businesses closing, and a general loss of confidence in the economy. But is there really less money now than there was two or twenty or fifty years ago? Are there really less resources? Have we used up more of the resources than are available to people on this planet? The answer is no. So where has all this money gone? Why is everyone poorer now than they were a few years ago? The answer is that money is not just a physical entity, a physical piece of paper. Money is also an energy that ebbs and flows. Money is an energy that manifests in confidence and expectation, in abundance that attracts more abundance.

Many of us are caught up in the fear cycle, watching the stock market drop and listening to the doom-and-gloom news. This is only perpetuating more of the same because our thoughts and emotions impress on our subconscious a focus for more of the same. Our world economy is in a spiraling state of panic and fear—fear of loss of money and lifestyle, which brings more loss of money and lifestyle.

In any economy, even during the Great Depression while the masses sunk lower and lower into financial fear, a select few were able to create great wealth. Some were able to rise above this collective conscious slump and use the energy of money and abundance to not only provide for themselves, but to provide in great abundance. It is this energy that we need to learn to tap into.

What Is Our Subconscious?

The origin of our being, our subconscious, the human conception of this and God, is a subjective matter. Some of us have traditional religious beliefs and some of us more metaphysical beliefs. If you have definite conceptions based on your religion or upbringing that don't fit into what appears to be a metaphysical or alternative viewpoint that I will be describing, please have an open mind and consider it. Regardless of what you believe, it will not affect the prosperity programming of your subconscious presented in this book and your ability to use your subconscious to enjoy and benefit from the fruits of life.

Imagine that God is the Universal energy, the white light source, one whole being or energy made up of love and joy and happiness, the Divine Source Energy—an energy that is omnipotent and can create all things and all experiences. But in order to really appreciate this love, joy, and happiness, God needed to look back at himself in different ways, through different experiences; and being one whole he could not do that. He then split off little parts of himself, little images of himself. These little images enable him to look back at himself. Each one can experience joy and love in different ways that could be experienced by the whole.

Each of us is one of these little individual images of God—an individual part of his energy, made in perfect duplicate to this energy, with all the same love and light, just in a miniature version. Now imagine that this little part of God within each of us is connected to our subconscious—this little part within us, made in his perfect image, with all the perfection that is God and yet individual. Our subconscious appears separate and individual, yet it is still part of God and remains connected to the whole. In the same way, cells of a body have different functions and can work independently, yet they have all the blueprint and knowledge and support from the whole body of which they are a part.

Now, imagine that some of us in this raw form of our subconscious energy, this miniature part of this Divine Source Energy, decided to experience life in a physical way; to experience love and joy and happiness but also to experience the lack of these emotions so that we can compare and appreciate them. Then some of us take the plunge to become a physical person. We are still connected to this Divine Source Energy through our subconscious and, as part of this energy, we have all the resources of the whole. We are able to connect through prayer, through meditation, and through love. In fact, we are continually connected on a soul level through our subconscious, and cared for and assisted through life.

Our physical body and conscious mind do not remember our source and our purpose in order that we may experience things as new, from which to gain a new perspective and thereby to learn. Yet, on a higher subconscious soul level, we have all the knowledge and all the supply from the great Divine Source Energy that God is.

What I have personally seen over and over is that our subconscious is connected to Source Energy. We are able to draw from, tap into, and manifest from this energy. Even though we are each working through life separately, we all draw from the same pool, the same endless supply of energy waiting to manifest all that we need and desire. As a whole entity, we are all benefitting from each other, learning and raising our collective consciousness together.

You may be saying, "What does any of this have to do with money?" Well, money is an energy that flows through us and around us. As we are part of this Universal God or Divine Source Energy, we can manifest anything and any experience through Source Energy. If what we desire requires money, then this energy of money will be manifested too. In fact, it is our soul purpose to experience joy and to live life in a rich and fulfilling way. It is our connection to the Divine Source Energy that is our supply of money, and not some person, job, or other external condition that may dissolve tomorrow. The external source is only the means through which our supply is given to us. The actual source is the Divine Source Energy.

My aim is to reconnect you to Divine Source Energy so that you may manifest your desires and the abundance you need to fulfill those desires.

How Our Subconscious Works

We Are Connected to Source Energy

If we are all connected to Source and, in fact, are ourselves miniature versions of this Divine Source Energy, then it is not too hard to understand that we too can manifest and create the things that we desire.

This Divine Source Energy is actually part of us, embedded inside each and every one of us, working automatically and perfectly through our subconscious. It is actually working for us all the time, right now. We don't have to do anything special to make it work; it continually manifests the things in our life that we are "asking" for. The catch is in the asking since it is not exactly done in the way you might think. This is what we need to concentrate on: learning to "ask" in the right way and programming our subconscious to bring us only the things that we do want and not the things we do not want.

Be Careful What You Ask For

Our subconscious is a perfectly automated machine whose job is not to question what we ask for, but rather to just bring it. It is like our personal computer where we place our order from the Divine Source, and whatever we order, big or small, good or ugly, will come to us. The subconscious does not turn around and say to us, "Do you really want that? Are you sure you are going to like that?" Our subconscious merely places the order as we request. Even if we have a sense of humor and are joking about what we want, our subconscious doesn't have a sense of humor and doesn't question; it just delivers.

The issue is that in incarnating on Earth, we have forgotten how to use our subconscious. It works perfectly, but we no longer know how to use it properly. Whatever we are thinking about, dreaming of, or focusing on will come to us. If you are thinking about a new car that you really want, daydream about it in a positive way. If you pay attention, the Universe will bring you an opportunity that will ultimately lead to your desire.

However, if and when you dream about this new car you are also thinking, "There is no way I could afford that," then you are impressing upon your subconscious a desire for more of the same—that is, to not be able to afford the car. If you see a friend with a similar car and become jealous of his ability to have that, you are again impressing upon your subconscious feelings of lack and jealousy and you will, in turn, receive back more lack and more reason to experience jealousy. Vibrations match vibrations.

There is also a positive side to this. In our quest to experience life, we need to see opposites in order to appreciate what we truly desire. How can we know what true love is if we have no experience of a lack of it? How can we know peace if we don't also know strife?

God Works in Mysterious Ways

They say God works in mysterious ways, and I am sure you have all seen examples of this. When we put it out there that we want something, be it through prayer or meditation, or just speaking or thinking of something, it will eventually come to us. But it usually doesn't come in exactly the way we think or plan it in our mind.

Don't Micromanage

As you start to develop your ability to ask your subconscious to bring you what you desire, don't ask for specific details or tell God (or Divine Source Energy) exactly how you want it delivered. Just put your desire out to Source and allow the Divine Source Energy to deliver. Start to look for little signs. Perhaps it will come through people that you will be introduced to, events that you will be drawn to, or little coincidences. Rarely will you be given the exact scenario you have in mind, but if you ask clearly without doubt, you will always be delivered the result.

The subconscious will not be responsive to you micromanaging every detail. You may actually even block what you want by thinking that it can only happen in a certain, specific way. You need to trust. Put in your request, then feel confident that not only will you receive your request shortly, but that it is already on its way. You can go about your business knowing that your request is about to arrive and that you have no doubt of its coming. Your subconscious, if left to its own devices, will always choose the best path for you.

Setting Goals

Where do you want to be this year, this month, or later this week? What dreams do you have? When you set a goal or envision a dream, this is the first step to manifesting it in your life. Sit and daydream for a moment. Visualize what your life will look like next year. Envision a cherished desire coming to fruition.

Daydreaming is actually very positive. The more clearly and detailed you can envision having what you want, the more quickly it will come to you. Back to that car you were visualizing. What color is it? Imagine driving it. Imagine what it would feel like to be behind the wheel, what your new car would smell like, how it responds to your commands. Imagine how wonderful you feel driving it. How happy you are to have the car of your dreams. Really feel this joyful emotion filling you up. Where do you want to go? Do you have your window down, your hair blowing in the breeze, taking tight turns along a cliff-side beach road? The more you can envision in specific detail and with positive emotion, the more quickly a path will open up to materialize your dream.

Part of the Team

Just for an exercise, put aside all your practical thoughts and religious beliefs and take an imaginary journey with me. Imagine that before we are born into this physical life, we are all God energies. We live in a place called heaven where we are surrounded by absolute beauty and bliss. In this place, we are each our own separate persona that we are today and are closely connected to everyone else that we love, admire, and cherish. We are separate individuals but also a part of this wonderful group of all energies, spirits, or souls that makes up the universal energy of God or the Divine Source Energy.

Although we continue to learn lessons and improve ourselves, we are not able to advance as quickly and as deeply as when we are in a physical body. So with a yearning to more deeply experience life, to experience joy more fully in a physical way, we decide that we are "going in." We are taking the plunge to join the physical world. Surrounded by loved ones, we plan our journey. Our loved ones rally around us as our support team, but they remain in heaven as part of the Divine Source Energy.

One very advanced soul agrees to be our main Spirit Guide, to be with us our entire physical life, to guide us through and be our connection to heaven. Other souls agree to stay close and offer advice in their areas of expertise. One soul will help us through our relationships, another will help us with our business decisions, and so forth, until we have a whole team of spirits backing us up. Some may advise us our entire life and some may stay only for as long as we need them. Some have been our parents or siblings in physical lives before. All are along for the journey to experience and learn through us. Of course God, the Divine Source Energy of which we are all a part, is watching over us, there to give help when we ask.

One of our main purposes here in the physical realm is to experience as much joy and happiness as possible. This joy is shared by our spirit guides and other souls that watch over us, as well as by the entire collective energy of souls and Divine Source Energy or God. Every time we experience joy in our lives, other souls revel in our well-being, feeling the joy and happiness that we feel, gathering close to us to soak in the physical joy that they cannot themselves create. Even though they can create joy in the non-physical world, this energy of physical joy is very special to them. Alternatively, when we experience guilt, fear, or sadness, these souls experience this along with us. They don't experience physical pain or the intensity of our sadness, but nevertheless they are affected by our sorrows.

Would this scenario change your attitude toward taking pleasure in life? Would it change how you feel about doing something for yourself without guilt? Will you take a day and do something really nice for yourself? Will you go to a spa or just sit and read a book? We've all indulged our desires at some point and judged ourselves negatively for it. Have you taken a vacation, only to come back to a pile of "work" and felt guilty about taking the time off? Have you felt selfish or guilty for having spent money on something for yourself? From this new perspective, you can see that in taking time for joy, you aren't being selfish, as your whole team enjoys these moments of pleasure. Alternatively, when you feel guilty or selfish for enjoying yourself, this can create sadness for your team as well.

Therefore, take that bit of time to pamper yourself, to treat yourself to a special event or that new outfit you've been looking at. Eat that chocolate truffle once in a while. Go out with your friends or turn off the phone and soak in a hot bath. Find that something every day that makes you feel warm and fuzzy, that makes you laugh, that makes you smile, and stop and appreciate the little joys in life because it is not just for yourself!

These moments when we are experiencing joy, when we are truly appreciating life, are the moments we are truly connected to the Divine Source Energy. This is what it feels like to be in sync, to be one with Source Energy. These are the moments we should strive to create.

This feeling of joy may even expand to those beyond yourself and your team. When we are happy and in moments of appreciation, people are attracted to us; they feel good being around this energy. Everyone wants to be around someone who is enjoying life and has a positive outlook.

What does all this have to do with money? Well, although money doesn't buy happiness, it can certainly provide us with some of the things that bring us moments of happiness. Money can give us the freedom to do the things we'd like to do, and it can afford us experiences we might like to have—all of which puts us closer to the moments of joy that are shared with everyone around us. I use this as an example to show you that money is not some evil, and that you should not feel greedy or selfish for desiring more money. If what you do with that money brings joy and appreciation for life, which connects you to your team and the Divine Source Energy, then this is a good use of this money energy.

That being said, I am not advising that you should go overboard and spend like crazy. In fact, this will not bring you the kind of real happiness that you strive for anyway. What I am saying is to cherish the time you spend with your loved ones, look to the positive side of everything you do, and stop to smell the roses along the way. Take the time to appreciate and give thanks for what is good in your life. If you want to splurge every so often or treat yourself to something special, do it. Enjoy yourself! Laughing and bringing yourself and others joy is probably the single most important thing you can do in life.

AAAA – Ask, Attention, Act, Appreciate

The first part of your job is to deliberately **ASK** your subconscious for the things you desire and to make a conscious effort to stop thinking and talking about the things you do not desire. As you ask, remember to be careful not to dwell on the lack of something rather than focusing on the desire to have something. If you dwell on the lack of something, it will in turn prevent or delay what you are asking for, as what you are really asking for is the lack of that thing. You must ask by thinking positively about something (some object or event you desire). Start to imagine having that object or experiencing that event, focusing on the happiness that it is bringing to you, feeling the positive emotions as you think about your desire. Imagine, in great detail, all the specifics of what it is you desire; what it feels like to have or experience it. Go over the emotions of how you will feel when you have this thing, imagining it in present tense. Visualize and feel it as if you already have it. When you deliberately manifest something, you do have it right now in the present. It may be waiting on the psychic plane to be delivered when you truly believe in it, but it is there and waiting for you.

Once you have asked your subconscious to deliver something to you, it is your job to sit back, be patient, and continue with your life, confidently knowing that your desire is being manifested.

After asking you now need to pay **ATTENTION.** Your desire may present itself to you in a different way than you are expecting and probably will. Therefore, pay attention to the little details and coincidences that appear to you. Your desire may be coming to you through a new contact, a new person at work, or an old friend you bump into. You may receive a new way to earn the money that you are asking for in order to obtain the thing that you have asked for. Put out some inquiries, some feelers, and then pay attention to things that come back to you.

Rarely does your desire just appear. Usually you are pointed in the right direction in which to obtain your desire, or your desire is given to you in several parts until you have the whole. You have to do some work here.

There is a well-known fable or joke that goes something like this: There is a priest living in a chapel on a little island. A great storm is forecast and everyone is warned to leave the island. Several men found a big fishing boat and all the villagers pile in. They tell the priest, "Leave the chapel and come with us in the boat." "Don't worry about me," the priest says. "I am going to stay here. I am a man of God and God will save me." So all the villagers leave the island by boat. Hearing that the priest is still on the island, the Coast Guard sends out a helicopter. The helicopter hovers overhead and throws down a rope to the priest. "Don't worry about me," the priest says as he tells the helicopter to leave. "I am going to stay here. I am a man of God and God will save me." A few hours later, a great hurricane hits and the priest is swept away to sea. He dies and goes to heaven. When he sees God on the other side he says, "What happened? I am a man of God. I thought you would come to rescue me!" to which God replied, "I sent you a boat and then I sent you a helicopter—what were you waiting for?"

The moral of this story is, when you ask for something you desire, you must pay attention and recognize what is being offered to you.

Next, when something is being offered, you need to **ACT,** as you must participate in receiving. For example, you may receive an invitation to an event that could bring you the necessary contact that will in turn bring your desire. However, you have to *act* and go to the event. How many chances and offerings do you need to get before you act on something that will bring about your desire? Keep a keen eye out and if an unexpected opportunity comes up, you should probably pursue it. Be active and look for opportunities (without forcing a certain way for your desire to come from a certain source). If an old friend comes out of nowhere, perhaps you should give them some time. Often you are offered your opportunity in return for giving service to another. In particular, watch out for ways in which you can help others. Again, don't expect that just because you helped someone that they will give you part of or the end result that you are hoping for. Just continue to participate in life and willingly and happily give service to others. You will be surprised at the doors it will open for you.

In doing something, you are showing the Universe that you are serious about your desire. You are confirming to your subconscious that, yes, you really do want to have this thing or this experience, and you are asking for more ways to present themselves so you can act on them.

Think about it. How can your desire be manifested? It is not going to just drop out of the sky into your lap. It is not going to appear from an obviously magical and spiritual source. It has to come via earthly physical means. It could present itself to you through channels that are already familiar, or it may not. Again, you should not be expecting and forcing a result from a particular person, job, or source. Not all the things you follow will pan out, but you may be surprised that most opportunities will carry some merit, even though it may not be to manifest the specific thing you are asking for right now.

Once your subconscious is given clear direction, it will automatically set about bringing you the thing that you desire. The Divine Source will deliver it to you in exactly the right time and exactly the right way for you. In fact, if you are clear regarding the intention and the end feeling of the desired item, you may in fact receive something better than you had envisioned.

When you have received the thing you are asking for, you need to give thanks and **APPRECIATE** what has been sent to you. In fact, you need to give thanks and appreciation before you receive what you are asking for. In giving your appreciation, you are affirming that you have total faith in the Divine Source Energy to deliver your desire. You are affirming that you understand that your desire is already manifested and on the psychic plane waiting to come to you. You are affirming that your subconscious is in total harmony with you and working perfectly and automatically. You are affirming that your subconscious will bring you signs and lead you in the right direction. You are affirming that you wish for more things to come to you that are in alignment with your desires and which you will appreciate.

Do not be disappointed if you don't get exactly what you want to start with, or you get only part of what you wanted. In feeling disappointed, you have defeated yourself. You are telling your subconscious that you desire more of what you are feeling, which is disappointment. So be grateful and thankful for every part that comes to you, and be confident in appreciation of what you will be given.

Start Spending, Stop Hoarding

Money is an energy. You need to start seeing money in that way and stop seeing it as a piece of paper. In a healthy economy, money circulates and the energy of money flows freely. A sick economy is when everyone hoards what they have and limits what they spend. There is no more money in a good economy, and there are no more supplies of things that people want—the only difference with a poor economy is the energy is not flowing smoothly. It has been slowed or stopped.

When you hold onto money, saving out of fear that you will need it (as you do not believe there will be more to follow), you are actually impressing that fear onto your subconscious and asking it to bring you more of the same vibration—that is, more of the vibration or emotion of fear and lack, of no money circulating to you, of more need to save, of there not being enough money. The subconscious does not question what you ask for; rather it just brings you the perfect match of the vibration you are sending out or "asking for," which is more of the same!

Money and other energies are meant to flow to us, from us, and freely through us. When you hold onto money in fear, you are stagnating the energy of money. When you start to retain this energy, you are artificially blocking money. By preventing money from flowing away from you, you are preventing it from flowing toward you as well. You are impressing upon your subconscious that you do not wish money to flow and that you wish the energy to be stopped. Of course, you get exactly what you ask for.

When you spend your money without regret and with appreciation for the things that the money is bringing to you, then you are impressing on your subconscious a desire to bring more money to you so that you may experience more of the vibration of happily spending—more of the vibration of the natural flow toward you.

Now, I am not saying that you should spend your money frivolously or simply for the sake of spending, as then again you are bringing more of the same energy back upon you. In other words, you will continue to engage in more frivolous spending that brings you little real joy and satisfaction. But do not feel guilty about treating yourself to something special. Feel thankful for what you have received and know that others are grateful for the energy of money that you flowed to their business.

There is truth to the Feng Shui belief that clutter stagnates energy, and clearing out clutter can bring you an increase in abundance and more money flowing to you. Things will flow to you when a space has been created for them. Literally clear out your closets and your desk of physical clutter. If you donate your unwanted things, especially to someone you know will appreciate it, then you are creating a void from which your new desire can be manifested. You are also giving to someone who will appreciate your gift, and this energy will return to you. If you hold on to an item of clothing just because it was expensive but you never wear it, you are impressing on your subconscious an energy of stagnation for both things and money. The energy of money and abundance is a flowing energy. In order to encourage the things you want to flow freely to you, you must show your subconscious that you allow things to flow freely from you to another.

It is important that you also donate money to others. This shows your subconscious that you trust in the Source Energy to continue to provide financially for you. Don't say, "But I don't have enough to donate anything right now, I will wait until I have more." This will impress on your subconscious to make sure you "don't have enough to donate anything right now" and will continue to keep you in this position that you are asking for. It is not the amount that is important. It is the act of giving. Give without regret or worry and not with the expectation that you will be repaid by your subconscious, for donating with reservation will bring you the same reservation back.

In addition to giving money, give of your time. In giving your time, you are impressing on your subconscious that you have plenty of time, and you will actually find that you have more time to yourself. Ask your subconscious how you can help others, and the answer will come to you. In helping others you will attract to you the help you would like. You will be surprised at the contacts you make while helping others, or perhaps you will gain some item or information that will put you closer to your desire.

If on the other hand, you say you cannot give as you cannot afford it or you don't have the time, your subconscious will set about receiving this that you have asked for and you will actually have the money taken away from you. You may not realize that the parking ticket you got and the unexpected bill you received are related to the money you didn't want to part with or the time you didn't have to help another. Sometimes the exact amount that you refuse to part with is taken away from you in the same amount in the form of a bill you were not expecting.

Money sitting under your mattress is a direct impression to your subconscious that you don't desire any money, as you don't desire to spend it, invest it, or donate it. It impresses upon your subconscious that you don't need money. Even safely investing your money is still circulating your money and allowing it to flow to others and back.

Debts: Get Out of the Cycle

Just the act of thinking about your debts, your lack of money, or how you are going to pay your bills in fact brings you more debt. This is the most challenging cycle to beat, especially in a difficult economy where you are bombarded with nothing but talk of lack—on the news, at work, and through friends. It is hard to get away from dwelling on lack and your bills. But here is how it works: when you look at a bill and automatically feel negative and start to think about it costing too much or there isn't enough to go around or how are you going to pay these bills, you are impressing on your subconscious to bring you more of the same vibration you are feeling. You are telling your subconscious that since you are dwelling on this matter, it is of importance to you and that you desire more of this frequency. As mentioned, our subconscious does not question if you really want this; it simply sets about to bring you more of what you are focusing on, which is that feeling. You then receive more bills in the mail and more feeling of lack and negativity, which again creates more until you are in the downward spiral of debts taking over your life and consuming your very being. When many people are doing the same thing as you, the entire economy starts to spiral into debt, worry, and negativity.

STOP!!!! To end this cycle, you must first stop thinking in this way. You cannot turn this around and start to receive abundance in your life until you change how you think. Stop unconsciously asking for more debt. I know this is much easier said than done, but remember, a positive thought is much more powerful than a negative thought. Every time a negative thought creeps in, catch it quickly and replace it with a positive thought. The positive ones will more than cancel out the negative ones.

Start asking for money to come into your life and for your bank accounts to fill up. Visualize this happening. However, if while you are thinking about this money coming in, your intent for this money is simply to pay off your debts, or to pay for something you believe you cannot afford, you are still impressing negativity on your subconscious. Your subconscious will hear that you need to have money to pay debts, and so you will receive more of the same vibration: a need to have money only to pay off debts. Even if your willpower is great enough to bring in additional money, it will also bring in the additional debt to fulfill what it is you are asking for. You might recall examples of this in your life—where you received additional income or money that you weren't expecting, only to have it come just in time to pay off some unexpected bill.

Next time you go to your mailbox, envision that it is going to be filled with envelopes with checks in them, or letters of news of abundance coming to you.

Imagine being happily surprised at where these checks came from—like places that you weren't expecting. Imagine your joy as you open your mail. Go overboard and really imagine your mailbox being stuffed and overflowing with these letters containing money and wonderful news. Feel the emotion of joy as this money comes in. Feeling the positive emotion of receiving/having what you want helps to manifest it.

Now, each time a bill comes in, I want you to take a moment and appreciate what it is that you have received. If it is a credit card statement, appreciate that you have the freedom to have a credit card. Imagine being able to go to a store knowing that you can make the purchases that make you happy, as well as those that provide for your needs. Notice items on your bill that gave you pleasure. Remember what a good time you had at that restaurant or how much you enjoyed wearing that new outfit. Then write your check happily, giving thanks that you are entrusted with this card and the convenience that it gives you.

If it is your mortgage or rent payment, give thanks for your home, what you love about your home, and that you are trusted by your bank or by your landlord. Do not think "How am I going to pay my rent/mortgage next month?" or "Am I going to lose this house?" When you pay your water bill, think for a second about how much you appreciated that hot shower you took this morning. Think about how much you enjoy your beautiful garden that you are able to water.

As you send out each bill, do so with thanks that you can pay it and not with disdain as to how much it just took out of your bank account and how little you have left. Learn to appreciate paying bills in the same way you appreciate giving a gift to someone. In this way you are telling your subconscious to bring you more money to allow you to give more thanks.

If the bill is for something that you dislike, and you feel you got nothing enjoyable in return, try to find some way that the experience makes you feel good. If you are paying a parking ticket, imagine all the times you got away with not getting a ticket. Laugh that this was the one time when you have gotten away with many more times. Or perhaps the money from the ticket is helping to provide city services for those in need. If it is something you just can't bring yourself to be grateful for, just give thanks that you have the means to satisfy all things that come up and resolve that you will not dwell on them.

In having this positive attitude about your debts, you are impressing on your subconscious to always bring you more than enough money to pay your bills; that you wish for more of this vibration of financial confidence, as the Divine Source will always provide for your needs.

If your attitude is "I always have enough to go around, all my needs and desires are always taken care of," then you shall attract more situations in your life that confirm this belief.

Connecting to Subconscious with a Pendant

We are constantly talking to our subconscious whether we realize it or not. This could be out loud, rehearsing prospective conversations with people in our head, talking to ourselves, etc. Even if you are not one to talk to yourself, you are always thinking, dreaming, and experiencing, all of which is "heard" by our subconscious.

If you are late to a meeting, worrying about whether or not you are going to get a close parking spot, chances are your subconscious is going to hear you worrying about and focusing your energy on that faraway parking space. It will then give you exactly what you were inadvertently asking for—a parking spot far away. However, if you are happily confident, thinking about that parking spot right in front and expecting it to be there, chances are that is what your subconscious is going to hear and that is what it is going to arrange.

As we go about our day-to-day living, we are bombarded with decisions, thoughts, hopes, and fears, all of which our subconscious picks up on. Once you understand how your subconscious works, you probably will try to make more of a conscious effort to give your subconscious only the thoughts of things you desire to manifest in your life.

This is much easier said than done! All of us relapse into "ordinary thinking," and this sometimes brings about events, people, or things that are not part of our desires. It is hard for us to differentiate between when we are actively talking to our subconscious about the things that we want to manifest and when we are passively allowing things to impress upon it that we do not want to manifest.

It is not generally our day-to-day experience to connect deliberately and clearly to our subconscious regarding the desires that we wish to manifest. At the start of your program (Day 1), I will teach you how to use an external object to clarify and intensify your desires to your subconscious. This object can be a pendant, a stone, a small crystal, a little trinket, etc. You are going to be wearing it or keeping it in your pocket for 30 days, so make sure this is an item that you don't mind having on you every day.

Now I do this with great caution and reservation. This object is only meant to be used as a temporary tool to help you obtain a stronger, clearer connection with your subconscious until such time as this becomes natural to you. It is not meant to be something that becomes your superstitious object or lucky charm that you become so reliant on that you feel you cannot manifest without it.

Connecting to your subconscious is the most natural instinct we were born with. Unfortunately, we have lost track of how to use it. This object is to help you to get back on track to direct your energy so that you can relearn what is your natural instinct. Therefore, after you have received your desired results with your object, it will be your goal to wean yourself off this until you develop the confidence to realize that this is still just an object, and that you no longer need it to connect with what is rightly yours.

There may be objects, things, or routines that you are already using, unbeknownst to you. People develop superstitious attachments that they believe are "lucky." There is no such thing as luck. There is no such thing as coincidence. Our life experience is as we make it, consciously or unconsciously. Often our superstitions are just something that we have placed between us and our desires because we do not believe in ourselves and our power directly. This program will help you to reclaim your power.

You are now ready to program your subconscious to its maximum potential for prosperity and abundance!

SECTION TWO

If you honestly and fully devote yourself to the few minutes a day that this program requires and diligently follow it, you will absolutely see remarkable results. In fact, I have so much faith in you that I am willing to give your money back if you do not experience results. So don't let me down, and more importantly, don't let yourself down. When you are ready to change your life for the better and to allow abundance in, you may proceed.

How To
Follow This Program

Section II is the 30-day program that will set your subconscious to automatically attract abundance. If you follow these day-to-day exercises, exactly as given, you will experience results.

Please note: It is not wise to share what you are doing each day with other people, at least until you have finished. You do not want your subconscious to be influenced by the criticism or critique of others, or by your own self-consciousness about their opinion. Just keep it under wraps until you are confidently producing the abundance you desire.

You will want to arrange an uninterrupted 30-day block where you can find a few minutes each day, around the same time. If you have to go out of town, make sure that you can commit to continuing this program while you are traveling.

The presentation of each daily exercise includes a blank space for you to write down your thoughts and insights. It is important that you do this. If you find you need additional space or you have to repeat certain days, you may add another notebook or extra pages. If you use an extra notebook, dedicate the use of this notebook to only this prosperity program.

You must follow the program every day, preferably around the same time each day. If you miss a day, you must go back and repeat the previous three days before you continue on. If you miss more than one day, you need to start over at the beginning (Day One). If you feel like you were not concentrating one day or were interrupted, just repeat that day again before going on to the next. For these reasons, the program may take you longer than 30 days to complete.

In order to get results, it is crucial for you to make the decision that you are willing to commit to this program for the full 30 days and to give it your all. If you follow this workbook with your full attention and dedication, it *will* increase your abundance.

"Today is the first day of the rest of your life,

Today start creating the life you really want..."

GETTING INTO THE ZONE

Find a time and a place that you will not be disturbed—ideally one that you can return to daily without interruption. I prefer early in the morning, rising before everyone else. However, any time of day is perfectly acceptable if that is more convenient for you. Your space can be either indoors or outdoors. Since I live in California where the weather is warm, I prefer outdoors in nature, but that may not be the best option for you. Creating a personal space is simply deciding upon a nice place where you feel comfortable. You may want to create a mini "altar" with a few objects, candles, and photos that put you in a good mood. If outdoors, it could be on a comfy seat by some special flowers. If the only place where you can find real privacy is the bathroom, that is fine too.

Sit comfortably. Turn off the phone and make sure you have privacy. I prefer quiet, but if you like soft music to relax, that is fine. I don't suggest lying in bed or in such a cozy chair that you are likely to fall asleep.

Now you are going to meditate to relax your body. If you have never done a meditation, don't be concerned. The whole point of this is simply to put yourself into a quiet, relaxed state.

Read the paragraph below and try to remember the gist of it. It is best if you can remember the meaning so that you can put this workbook down while you are doing the exercise. You do not need to read this out loud, nor say this word for word, as you do the other sections of this workbook. You will be envisioning this and talking silently in your head.

Sit quietly and relax with your feet uncrossed and flat on the floor. Place your hands, palms up, on your lap. Concentrate on your breathing, envisioning taking in deep breaths of positive energy through your nose and releasing negative energy through your mouth. Now, I want you to envision a beautiful orb or ball of light like a bright white star in the sky, shining down on you. It comes closer and closer to you until it is hovering above your head. Imagine this orb sending healing and protective white light energy, in the highest of goodness. Imagine this white light coming from this orb, shining down on your head and then going over your shoulders and continuing down your body, slowly over each part, all the way to your toes. As you imagine this white light traveling down your body, it brings healing and protective energy, which feels like warm sunshine on your body. It relaxes each part that it touches. Feel each part of your body relaxing until you are completely enveloped in this white light of protection. You are now in a bubble of white light and only good energies can come into your space.

DAY 1

Starting My New Life of Abundance

Remember to do "Getting into the Zone" before you start.

Today we are going to program your pendant. You can use any object: a piece of jewelry, a stone, a small crystal, a charm, some kind of trinket, etc. You are going to wear or carry this for at least the 30-day program, so be sure it is something that you don't mind having on you every day. It can be concealed in your pocket, worn as a necklace, bracelet, etc. The idea is that it is in your energy (aura), close to your body. After the program, you may continue to use this object or you may discard it.

1. In a place that is comfortable to you and that you are not going to be disturbed, stand with your feet slightly apart, relaxed and with equal weight on each foot.

2. Place this workbook open to that day's page, where you can easily read it while standing.

3. Hold the pendant or object you have chosen in your right hand and rub it gently between your fingers. If you are left-handed or this is easier, it is perfectly fine to use your left hand. However, we are always going to use the same hand each day and stand in the same way—this is now your **"Power Position."**

4. As you do this, you may feel an energy surge that may make you rotate, lean, or move. Just go with it. Allow your weight to shift or your body to move around. If you feel like standing still, that is fine too.

5. While you are rubbing your object, read the following paragraph out loud:

I am open to the Divine Source Energy. My subconscious has a perfect connection to the Divine Source Energy and manifests to me all my desires in the highest of goodness. Whenever I rub this pendant (charm, stone, etc.), I am clarifying the connection between my subconscious and the Divine Source Energy. I am clarifying the connection between my conscious thinking mind and my subconscious, and whatever my conscious mind desires my subconscious will deliver from the Divine Source Energy. I will be directed to ask for only persons, things, and events that are in my highest of goodness and that are part of my Divine Plan. All my desires will manifest quickly and clearly and in the highest of goodness. (You may replace the phrase "Divine Source Energy" with "God" if you prefer.)

You may now sit, or whatever feels relaxed and comfortable to you. Take a moment to reflect and meditate on this paragraph, asking what it means to you. Write down any insights that you have or reword it into what is meaningful to you.

_____

_____

_____

Now pick up your pendant again, stand, and take your Power Position. While rubbing your pendant, read the following paragraph out loud:

> *Today, _____ [fill in today's date], I am starting my new life of abundance, happiness, and joy. Today and from now on, I am connected to the Divine Source Energy. Today and from now on, I will follow my Divine Life Path. Today and from now on, I will connect clearly with my subconscious. Today and from now on, I will only think thoughts that attract people, things, and experiences to me that are in my highest of goodness. Today and from now on, I will allow abundance to flow freely to me. I now accept the great wealth that is mine by Divine Right.*

Take a moment to meditate on this second paragraph, asking what it means to you. Write down any insights that you have or reword it into what is meaningful to you.

DAY 2

I Am Part of God,
the Divine Source Energy

DAY 2

Remember to do "Getting into the Zone" before you start.

Stand in your Power Position. While holding and rubbing your pendant, read the following paragraph out loud:

I have always been a part of God, part of the Divine Source Energy. When I chose to incarnate on this Earth and become a physical being, I brought with me, deep inside my subconscious, my little part of the Divine Source Energy or God spark, and through this I remain connected to the Source as a whole. I am made in the perfect image of God because I am part of God. God, the Divine Source Energy, is all-powerful, all-giving, all-knowing, and can create all that I need or desire. Since I am a part of this Divine Source Energy, I too have all the powers of the Divine Source. Since I am part of God, I deserve all the abundance and all the happiness that the Universe can offer. I am now open to receiving the abundance that is mine by Divine Right. I now allow money to flow freely to me.

Take a moment to reflect and meditate on this paragraph, asking what it means to you. Write down any insights that you have or reword it into what is meaningful to you.

DAY 3

I Am the Source of My Abundance

Remember to do "Getting into the Zone" before you start.

Stand in your Power Position. While holding and rubbing your pendant, read the following paragraph out loud:

> *I am the source of my abundance. My God spark or little part of Divine Source Energy is within my subconscious and works automatically and perfectly, all the time. Whatever my conscious mind desires, my subconscious mind will deliver to me, on time and in the perfect way. I live in confidence that anything I desire, I will manifest. Anything I think upon, focus upon, or ask for, I will manifest. Since I am part of the Divine Source and the Divine Source is the creator of all that I desire, then I am the source of all that I desire. I shall only ask for or focus upon those things that bring happiness to my life, and I shall not speak of or dwell on anything negative. I now ask my subconscious to provide me with financial abundance in the highest of goodness. I now allow money to flow freely to me.*

Take a moment to reflect and meditate on this paragraph, asking what it means to you. Write down any insights that you have or reword it into what is meaningful to you.

_____

_____

_____

_____

_____

_____

_____

_____

_____

DAY 4

My Divine Life Plan

Remember to do "Getting into the Zone" before you start.

We all have a Divine Life Plan that is set forth for us before we incarnate and which we participate in choosing. Imagine that before you were born, you and the Divine Source Energy decided what you were to learn in this life and how you were to contribute to humankind. You came to Earth and promptly forgot all of this in your conscious mind. However, your subconscious mind, which remains connected to the Divine Source, is all-knowing and holds the blueprint to your Divine Life Plan.

Look back through the themes in your life to try to figure out what your true purpose might be. What are your hobbies? What are you good at? What recurring themes are in your life? What would you love to do if you didn't have to work? Perhaps your life purpose is to help people in some way. Do people keep coming to you for advice? Do situations keep coming up in your life where you take care of someone? Perhaps your life plan is to teach or to heal. Perhaps your life purpose is to build or create. Perhaps your purpose is to lead by example. It may be something completely different from how you earn your living, and often it is.

Today I want you to meditate on this and write down any recurring themes in your life. Ask what these may have to do with your Divine Life Plan. Write down your hobbies, your life passions and desires, and anything that comes to you that you have an inclination may be related to your life's purpose.

Meditate on what your Divine Life Plan is and write down your insights:

_____

_____

Now stand in your Power Position. While holding and rubbing your pendant, read the following paragraph out loud:

Before I incarnated into this life, there was a Divine Plan set forth for my life. This plan was designed by the Divine Source and myself and is in the highest of goodness for my soul's purpose. I may have wandered off track of my Divine Plan, but from this day forth, I submit to my subconscious to point me in the right direction of my Divine purpose. I now release all debts, all people, and all things that are not part of my Divine Plan and I ask that they release me. I know that in living my Divine Plan, I shall experience happiness and abundance. I know that part of my Divine Plan is to experience the joys of life and that this includes the financial freedom to enjoy all that I wish to experience. I ask that I may live my Divine Plan and follow the work that I am meant to do, immediately and in my highest of goodness.

Take a moment to reflect and meditate on this paragraph, asking what it means to you. Write down any insights that you have or reword it into what is meaningful to you.

DAY 5

I Dispel Any Negative
Beliefs I Hold About Money

Remember to do "Getting into the Zone" before you start.

Stand in your Power Position. While holding and rubbing your pendant, read the following paragraph out loud:

I reject any misunderstanding that money is evil and that poverty or striving is somehow good for the soul. I now know the truth: that my soul is meant to experience wealth, health, happiness, and abundance. I reject debt, worry, and struggling financially and I accept wealth into my life. I now know that the Divine Source Energy is the creator of all abundance and that I am part of this Divine Source Energy and therefore my subconscious has access to all that I desire. It is part of my Divine Plan that I be successful financially and be blessed with wealth and abundance. I now allow wealth and abundance to flow into my life immediately, easily, and in the highest of goodness. I see my bank accounts overflowing. I see checks coming to me in unexpected ways. I see cash flowing freely to me. I feel good about the energy of money and attract this goodness to me.

Take a moment to reflect and meditate on this paragraph, asking what it means to you. Write down any insights that you have or reword it into what is meaningful to you.

DAY 6

The Purpose of Life Is Joy

Remember to do "Getting into the Zone" before you start.

Stand in your Power Position. While holding and rubbing your pendant, read the following paragraph out loud:

The purpose of my life is to experience joy. The purpose of my creation was so that the Divine Source Energy could experience the physical world and physical emotion through me. Through me and through my experiences, the collective consciousness of humankind can grow. When I experience Joy, I am allowing the Divine Source Energy to share the physical feelings of Joy through me. Since all others are also connected to Divine Source Energy, they share these experiences of Joy. Therefore I am not selfish or indulgent in my search for Joy, as it is my soul's purpose. I allow financial abundance in my life, so that there are no obstacles to life's experiences that bring me Joy. I now allow myself all the pleasures of life and ask that the means shall be presented to me, immediately, easily, and in the highest of goodness. I ask that financial abundance flow to me immediately and effortlessly.

Take a moment to reflect and meditate on this paragraph, asking what it means to you. Write down any insights that you have or reword it into what is meaningful to you.

DAY 7

Wealth Is Every Person's Right

Remember to do "Getting into the Zone" before you start.

Stand in your Power Position. While holding and rubbing your pendant, read the following paragraph out loud:

Wealth is every person's right. Every person is born from the Divine Source with access to wealth, happiness, and abundance. Wealth is the natural, intended way. I may have wandered from my path and allowed false interpretations to convince me that I am not worthy of wealth. I may have chosen to experience lack, but this is not the natural way. I now know the truth, that wealth is my right and my destiny and part of my Divine Life Plan. Wealth is my right and the right of every person. I now put any false beliefs behind me and honor my Divine Life Plan and allow wealth to come to me. The wealth that is mine by Divine Right and waiting for me now comes to me immediately and in perfect ways, in my highest of goodness. I experience money flowing to me in unexpected ways, and I will allow a great abundance of wealth to come to me.

Take a moment to reflect and meditate on this paragraph, asking what it means to you. Write down any insights that you have or reword it into what is meaningful to you.

DAY 8

Meeting More Than My Needs

Today you are going to write down all your sources of income and all your monthly expenses.

Let's start with the first column for "INCOME." Under the "OLD" heading, place your current monthly income sources and total them. This should be your job, any commissions, and payments that others give you (child support, alimony, social security, etc.). If this varies, place an average for the last few months.

Now we are going to add more to each of these "INCOME" amounts. You are also going to add new sources that you envision for "INCOME." So, under "NEW" add more money to your income amounts and add new sources of income. Make these numbers as big as you would like them to be, but they need to be believable to you. You can envision these numbers as big as you can bring yourself to believe, right now. Your belief is your only limiting factor. For instance, you may believe that you can find a new source of revenue, but you may have a hard time believing that your salary itself could increase. Place the largest amounts here that you honestly think are possible within the next few months.

In the section entitled "SPENDING," under "WAS" place your previous monthly expenses, bills, and other things you spend money on and total them. Under "WILL BE" place what you are going to be spending each month. On your bills and monthly expenses, you want to add a little more than you currently owe. For your credit cards, add on 10%, so that you have more than enough money to pay off your debts, even so much that you can pay them off more quickly. Under your house rent or mortgage add 10% so that you can more than cover your mortgage and you can add back the rest to your house.

You will see that at the top of the "SPENDING" category there is an item called "Pleasure expenses." You need to start putting yourself and your ability to enjoy life at the top of your priorities. This should be at least 10% of your new total income. (I.e., if the new total income you envision is $4000 per month, you should list at least $400 per month to spend on pleasurable things for yourself.) Really this item should be a lot more than 10%, so push the limit until your mind finds it too hard to believe.

The second item under "SPENDING" is "Charity/helping others." You need to start allowing money to be spent on others. In order for money to flow to you, it must flow from you first. Again, put 10% of your new income here and make a commitment to spend that freely and without regret.

If you already feel like you have just enough income to barely make your expenses with nothing to spare, don't worry about it—simply put more income in your "NEW" column. This exercise is not about dwelling on your current lack. Once you have written down your old bills and expenses, just trust that the money will be there to cover them and much, much more.

Make sure that you can envision a believable enough income that you have a large amount in the "Leftover Income" total at the bottom.

MONTHLY INCOME/EXPENSES

INCOME	OLD	NEW	SPENDING	WAS	WILL BE
Income source 1	_____	_____	Pleasure expenses	_____	_____
Income source 2	_____	_____	Charity/helping others	_____	_____
Income source 3	_____	_____	House rent/mortgage	_____	_____
Other	_____	_____	Utilities	_____	_____
New		_____	Other house bills	_____	_____
New		_____	Insurance	_____	_____
			Health	_____	_____
Total Income	_____	_____	Cars	_____	_____
			School	_____	_____
			Credit cards	_____	_____
			_____	_____	_____
			_____	_____	_____
			_____	_____	_____
			_____	_____	_____
			_____	_____	_____
			_____	_____	_____
			_____	_____	_____
			_____	_____	_____
			_____	_____	_____
			Total Spending	_____	_____
			Total Leftover Income	$_____	_____

If you didn't already do "Getting into the Zone" then do it now.

Stand in your Power Position. While holding and rubbing your pendant, read the following paragraph out loud:

I will not dwell on my expenses. I draw all that I need and desire from the Divine Source, and I will always receive everything that I ask for. I trust in the Divine Source to bring me the financial abundance that I desire to pay more than my expenses and to provide me with the means to experience all the pleasures of life. I am now ready to allow my life to overflow with abundance. I am now ready to receive the money that is mine by Divine Right and is ready and waiting for me to manifest in my life. I make a commitment to share this abundance, for as I give, I will receive. As I pay my expenses, I will write my checks happily and be thankful for the abundance that allows me to pay my bills easily. I present this list of needs to my subconscious and ask that these needs be met. I trust that the Divine Source is my unlimited supply and that all I need to do is ask. I will not try to manipulate the way in which this abundance will come to me; I just trust in the Divine Source and give thanks, as it is already here.

Take a moment to reflect and meditate on this paragraph, asking what it means to you. Write down any insights that you have or reword it into what is meaningful to you.

DAY 9

I Am My Word

Remember to do "Getting into the Zone" before you start.

Stand in your Power Position. While holding and rubbing your pendant, read the following paragraph out loud:

I am my word. What I speak to myself and especially out loud will manifest in my life. The Divine Source will deliver to me whatever I ask for, focus upon, and speak. Therefore I will only speak of abundance and joy. I will not talk of lack, nor will I worry nor dwell on financial problems. Whenever I am tempted to speak of lack, I will replace these negative thoughts quickly with positive thoughts of the abundance that is mine by Divine Right. I remember that through my subconscious, I am connected to the Divine Source and therefore connected to all the abundance I desire. I will make a conscious effort to speak of abundance every day.

Take a moment to reflect and meditate on this paragraph, asking what it means to you. Write down any insights that you have or reword it into what is meaningful to you.

DAY 9

At the end of the day, reflect on when you deliberately talked about abundance in a positive way. Write down your findings.

DAY 10

I Do Not Look to the Outside But Within

DAY 10

Remember to do "Getting into the Zone" before you start.

Stand in your Power Position. While holding and rubbing your pendant, read the following paragraph out loud:

The Divine Source Energy is the only source I will look to. My job, my clients, and my physical income sources are only methods that Divine Source uses to bring my abundance to me, but they are not the source themselves. The Divine Source Energy works in mysterious ways and delivers to me all that I ask for, in perfect timing and in perfect ways. I shall not try to manipulate from where I am receiving my requests. Rather, I shall ask my subconscious for what I want and then I shall trust that it is coming to me from the Divine Source. I shall choose my work in the way it gives me pleasure and in the way I provide service to others. I shall not try to force my desires from any person, job, or thing. I trust in the Divine Source Energy to manifest my abundance through the perfect channels, in the highest of goodness. I now ask my subconscious to send me an abundance of checks and cash. I will not focus on what paths it will follow to get to me. I trust that it is coming to me from the sources that the Divine Source Energy chooses. I give thanks for this abundance, as it is already being manifested right now.

Take a moment to reflect and meditate on this paragraph, asking what it means to you. Write down any insights that you have or reword it into what is meaningful to you.

DAY 11

Do What I Love and Love What I Do

Remember to do "Getting into the Zone" before you start.

Stand in your Power Position. While holding and rubbing your pendant, read the following paragraph out loud:

I will do what I love and love what I do. I know that the things I love to do in life and the things that bring me the most joy must be part of my Divine Plan. It is also part of my Divine Plan that when I pursue the things that I love, I will receive abundance in my life. Therefore I will not worry about the source of my abundance; rather I will seek out what I love to do and the ways that I can be of service to others. I look at my hobbies and pastimes and I focus on my dreams. I focus on how I would like to spend my days. I impress upon my subconscious to make my dreams a reality. I will rely on the Divine Source Energy to provide abundantly for all my desires, and I shall occupy my mind in the pursuit of happiness.

Take a moment to reflect and meditate on this paragraph, asking what it means to you. Write down any insights that you have or reword it into what is meaningful to you.

DAY 12

Setting My Goals

DAY 12

Remember to do "Getting into the Zone" before you start.

Write down what you would like to be doing, earning, and experiencing: this week, in one month, in six months, in one year, and in ten years. Meditate on these goals. Then stand in your Power Position and while holding and rubbing your pendant, read each goal you have written and the timeline out loud.

My goals this week

_____

_____

_____

My goals in one month

_____

_____

_____

My goals in six months

_____

_____

_____

My goals in one year

_____

_____

_____

My goals in ten years

_____

_____

_____

Stand in your Power Position. While holding and rubbing your pendant, read the following paragraph out loud:

> *As I set my goals, my subconscious draws from the Divine Source Energy all that is necessary to complete these goals, in the perfect ways and in the perfect time. I shall not focus on details of how I shall accomplish these goals. I shall rely on the Divine Source Energy entirely and I shall only focus on the end results. All that I desire to do, I shall accomplish, if these aims are in my highest of goodness and I trust in the Divine Source. As I accomplish each goal, I shall be thankful and I will be rewarded with happiness and financial abundance. I shall then happily set another higher goal.*

Take a moment to reflect and meditate on this paragraph, asking what it means to you. Write down any insights that you have or reword it into what is meaningful to you.

_____

_____

_____

_____

_____

_____

_____

_____

_____

_____

DAY 13

My Creative Space

Choose a place where you can keep pictures and cutouts where they won't be disturbed. For example, this can be a corkboard by your office desk, the top of a dresser, a bookshelf, a special box, or the meditation space you are using.

Now place pictures, photos, magazine clippings, or notes that represent your desires. These desires can and should be monetary objects, such as a boat, a car, a dream house. You may also use a dollar ($) amount written on a piece of paper. Perhaps it is a picture of a beach in Hawaii that you long to visit. Be selfish here. This is where you put things to bring *you* joy.

When you look at these objects, feel the joy of having them. Do not let yourself feel envy of others when you look at them. Do not feel disappointed that you don't yet have this thing. Do not put a monetary amount on a piece of paper if it represents money you need for a specific bill and it makes you feel upset when you look at it. Money should not be desired simply to pay your expenses but to give you an excess to spend for your happiness.

It is good if this space is displayed where you can glance at it several times a day, such as by your desk.

Now you are going to make a concentrated effort to spend a few minutes several times a day, dreaming about the objects on your display. For each item imagine having it, driving it, using it, enjoying it, and being thankful for it. You should continue to add items as they appeal to you. Only put as many items on display as you have time to focus on.

Make a list below of items that you have placed in your creative space and any additional items you intend to focus on:

DAY 13

If you didn't already do "Getting into the Zone" then do it now.

Stand in your Power Position. While holding and rubbing your pendant, read the following paragraph out loud:

As I dream with joy about the things that I want to manifest in my life, my subconscious will deliver, from the Divine Source, these things in the perfect way and in my highest of goodness. I submit to my subconscious all the items I have placed in my creative space and any other items or desires I add to that space. I do not question how these things will appear in my life, and I do not try to control the way that they will come to me. I am grateful for my connection to the Divine Source Energy and know that all I desire, ask for, or focus upon will be given to me. All I need do is impress them upon my subconscious, and my subconscious will automatically and perfectly deliver them to me.

Take a moment to reflect and meditate on this paragraph, asking what it means to you. Write down any insights that you have or reword it into what is meaningful to you.

Now take your pendant and rub it on your list of your desires. As you run your pendant over this list repeat:

These objects and desires are now impressed upon my subconscious, and my subconscious will deliver these to me easily and immediately. I give thanks for these things, as they are already mine.

DAY 14

Help Me to Recognize Signs

You have to be watching carefully and willing to participate in the manifestation that is coming to you.

For instance, let's take Bill who worked in a sales position where he received commissions. Bill wished to have sufficient money to be able to buy a sailboat. His dream is to be able to go sailing on the weekends. He was focused on getting more sales commissions in order to get the sailboat of his dreams. One day Bill passed up going to a luncheon in the hope of receiving an important sales call for a large commission. What Bill didn't know was that if he had gone to lunch, he would have met his supervisor's son, who had just joined a beach club. The son had been given the loan of a very nice sailboat, but he didn't know the first thing about sailing. Here was Bill's opportunity to go sailing every weekend and have the boat practically to himself in exchange for giving the odd lesson. Bill didn't realize that he passed up the opportunity, and he didn't find out until months later when the son had already made other arrangements. Bill was too focused on the sales call and how he thought he would steer the end result. Unfortunately, Bill prevented his subconscious from bringing his desire in the most perfect way.

Therefore, instead of trying to force the direction that you will make money to have something, you need to concentrate on your desire, on the end result. Then just relax and look for the little signs that you are sent.

If you didn't already do "Getting into the Zone" then do it now.

Stand in your Power Position. While holding and rubbing your pendant, read the following paragraph out loud:

As I ask for my desires, I trust in the Divine Source to fulfill my desires in perfect ways. I will not force the sources of my income. I will not look to my work or any person for money. I simply ask and trust. I am now aware of the messages I receive from my subconscious and my guidance system. I relax in the knowledge that my desires are being taken care of and are coming to me quickly and by the right means for me. I am aware and attuned, so that I recognize the signs that are being given to me. I am open to and recognize the help that I am being given.

Take a moment to reflect and meditate on this paragraph, asking what it means to you. Write down any insights that you have or reword it into what is meaningful to you.

DAY 15

Manifest Something Small

Practice manifesting small things in your life. For instance, believe and expect a parking space right in front of where you are going. If it is not there right away, hang out just a couple of minutes, have faith, and it will be there. Then give thanks to Divine Source and smile to yourself. Or imagine the latte you would like to manifest. Imagine enjoying drinking it, how it tastes and smells, and then put it out of your mind. When it comes to you, maybe not now, maybe later in the day, give thanks and smile. Imagine an extra $5 or $20 bill coming to you today in an unexpected way. When it comes, smile and give thanks to Divine Source and appreciate that you are manifesting.

Practice this every day. Start with small things and then believe in bigger and better things.

If you didn't already do "Getting into the Zone" then do it now.

Think of three small things you will expect to manifest today. Write these items in the blank space in the paragraph below. Then stand in your Power Position. While holding and rubbing your pendant, read the following paragraph out loud:

> *I trust in Divine Source to bring all my desires into my life. I am now confident that anything that I ask for, big or small, will be instantly and correctly manifested in my life. My subconscious works perfectly, bringing all my desires to me instantly and in perfect ways. Today I will manifest*
>
> _____.

Take a moment to reflect and meditate on this paragraph, asking what it means to you. Write down any insights that you have or reword it into what is meaningful to you.

DAY 15

At the end of the day, write down at least three small things you expected and manifested today.

DAY 16

Be Thankful

Every day find something that you are grateful for. When I wake up in the morning, I step outside and look at the garden and the mountains, listen to the birds, and I give thanks for the beautiful nature around me. I spend a few moments being thankful for and appreciating all the wonderful things in my life. Being thankful for something automatically brings more things to you to be thankful for, for your subconscious attracts more of the same. Get into the habit of instructing your subconscious to bring you more of the same good things and to avoid more of the same bad things by concentrating on what you appreciate. As you go through your day, smile at the things you enjoy and say a little thank you.

If you didn't already do "Getting into the Zone" then do it now.

Stand in your Power Position. While holding and rubbing your pendant, read the following paragraph out loud:

> *I give thanks for the wonderful things in my life that I now know I have received from the Divine Source. I am grateful for the things, the people, and the experiences in my life that give me pleasure. I give thanks that I am connected to the Divine Source that provides all these wonderful things to me. I am grateful for the financial abundance that I have received, which has allowed me to afford these pleasures. I am grateful for the financial abundance that is coming to me. I am thankful that my cups are now overflowing. I am thankful for the comfort in knowing that all I desire is now instantly manifested in my life.*

Today I am grateful for:

DAY 17

Plenty to Go Around

DAY 17

Remember to do "Getting into the Zone" before you start.

Stand in your Power Position. While holding and rubbing your pendant, read the following paragraph out loud:

Anything that I desire and is in my highest of goodness will not take away from another who wants the same. The Divine Source Energy is an omnipotent source with unlimited resources that provides everything that everyone desires, without taking away from another. There is no lack in the world. Lack is only created by ones who are asking for the experience of lack. I do not need this experience and I reject lack in my life. I am confident that the Divine Source Energy will provide all that I desire and much more. There is no limit to what I may choose to experience. I choose to receive checks in my mailbox. I choose to receive unexpected amounts of cash. I choose to have more money than I need or ask for. As I receive financial abundance, I return financial abundance to circulation and I ask for abundance for all humankind.

Take a moment to reflect and meditate on this paragraph, asking what it means to you. Write down any insights that you have or reword it into what is meaningful to you.

DAY 18

Don't Covet Thy Neighbor's Possessions

Don't be jealous or envious of another, for in doing so you are telling your subconscious to continue to give yourself the lack of what you envy. If you see someone else with an object that you would like to have, give thanks that they have it because if they can manifest something, so can you.

Remember to do "Getting into the Zone" before you start.

Stand in your Power Position. While holding and rubbing your pendant, read the following paragraph out loud:

As I look upon the success or the possessions of another, I now appreciate and give thanks, for I know that if they can manifest such an object or result then it is possible for me to manifest similarly. Even if I harbor ill feelings toward this person, I now understand that in appreciating another's well-being, I am sending my subconscious the message to bring me similar experiences. From now on, I will stop to appreciate and give thanks for the blessings of others. I am thankful for the financial success of_____ [name people] and I ask for more abundance for them, as in doing so I am asking for abundance for myself. As I see and admire others, I now allow my subconscious to bring to me those objects of my desires, instantly and in perfect ways.

Take a moment to reflect and meditate on this paragraph, asking what it means to you. Write down any insights that you have or reword it into what is meaningful to you.

_____

_____

_____

_____

_____

_____

_____

_____

_____

_____

_____

DAY 19

Smile

Remember to do "Getting into the Zone" before you start.

Stand in your Power Position. While holding and rubbing your pendant, read the following paragraph out loud:

As I go through my day, I will make a conscious effort to smile more. I will smile to myself as I notice things that I appreciate and give thanks for. I will smile as I notice the blessings of others. I will smile at friends and acquaintances and, most importantly, I will smile at strangers. If I see a person in need, begging on a street corner, I will not look at them with pity, as in doing so I am offering them more lack. I will make an effort to smile at them and to take a second to imagine their life greatly improved. As I smile upon others and ask for their well-being, I am in turn asking for my well-being, as we are all connected through the Divine Source.

Take a moment to reflect and meditate on this paragraph, asking what it means to you. Write down any insights that you have or reword it into what is meaningful to you.

DAY 20

We Are All Connected

Remember to do "Getting into the Zone" before you start.

Stand in your Power Position. While holding and rubbing your pendant, read the following paragraph out loud:

I am connected to the Divine Source Energy and I am in fact a part of the Divine Source Energy. All other people are also connected to Divine Source Energy and are a part of Divine Source Energy. Everything I do affects them, and everything they do affects me. When I think of abundance, I attract abundance, and since we are all connected, we all benefit. When I wish for abundance for others, it also benefits me. Together we can raise the consciousness of the Universe, so that we may overcome issues of poverty and lack and bring abundance to all. The Divine Source has unlimited resources and unlimited powers. I now ask to be showered with financial abundance, and in doing so I am providing abundance to all humankind.

Take a moment to reflect and meditate on this paragraph, asking what it means to you. Write down any insights that you have or reword it into what is meaningful to you.

DAY 21

Take the Leap of Faith,
Break the Fear Cycle

Remember to do "Getting into the Zone" before you start.

Stand in your Power Position. While holding and rubbing your pendant, read the following paragraph out loud:

I believe in my subconscious and my connection to Divine Source Energy and trust that everything I need or desire will always be manifested from the Divine Source. Sometimes decisions in my life require great faith and trust. Sometimes in the past I have stayed put, out of fear. I now put my faith in the Divine Source that I shall be shown my Divine Life Plan and be given all that I need to accomplish this. I trust in my subconscious. I shall make the leaps of faith that are required, and I shall no longer live in fear. I have faith that abundance is delivered to me instantly and appears in my life now, as I ask for it. I do not worry about circumstances of money but will live my life for joy and trust that the Divine Source will provide all that I need and ask for.

Take a moment to reflect and meditate on this paragraph, asking what it means to you. Write down any insights that you have or reword it into what is meaningful to you.

DAY 22

All Problems Are Life Lessons

It is on the path to success that we often find the most satisfaction. It is the creative process of manifesting something. It is in the little problems that we encounter along the way that we learn and accomplish more. When we overcome an obstacle or problem, we are often more proud of the end result. Sometimes it is in experiencing the opposite of something that we realize and create our desire. We experience strife in order to more fully appreciate joy. We encounter bumps along the road so that we can better appreciate the destination or end result.

Remember to do "Getting into the Zone" before you start.

Stand in your Power Position. While holding and rubbing your pendant, read the following paragraph out loud:

I now review my life, my problems, and my financial struggles. I understand that these are temporary situations that are brought to me as learning lessons. I am free from all "problems" and I meet my life lessons with enthusiasm. Where my lesson is to learn how to appreciate things, I now appreciate and give thanks. Where my lesson is to learn patience, I now practice patience. Where my lesson is to love myself and allow myself to receive love, I now love myself and receive love. Where my lesson is to allow myself to receive abundance, I now understand my lesson and I allow abundance to flow freely in my life. I will never again feel the restraint of financial conditions. I have learned my lessons and I know that it is I who allows this abundance to come to me. I now live my life in abundance, and money comes to me effortlessly and immediately.

Take a moment to reflect and meditate on this paragraph, asking what it means to you. Write down any insights that you have or reword it into what is meaningful to you.

DAY 23

Live in the Now

Remember to do "Getting into the Zone" before you start.

Stand in your Power Position. While holding and rubbing your pendant, read the following paragraph out loud:

My life starts right now, today, in this moment. I now live my life moment by moment. I will not dwell on the past, as I cannot change it. I will not put my life on hold until sometime in the future. I start right now, living every moment and enjoying every moment. I manifest right now the abundance that I want in my life. I do all the things that I wish to do. I do not ponder or plan for the future; rather I put it into action right now. I start right now in this moment, appreciating all that I have and all that is being manifested for me. I have abundance right now, immediately, and more is manifested instantly upon my asking for it. I live today with faith and abundance.

Take a moment to reflect and meditate on this paragraph, asking what it means to you. Write down any insights that you have or reword it into what is meaningful to you.

DAY 24

Start Spending, Stop Hoarding

DAY 24

Remember to do "Getting into the Zone" before you start.

Stand in your Power Position. While holding and rubbing your pendant, read the following paragraph out loud:

I give freely now. I spend freely on myself and others and I gladly pay my expenses. I will not be frivolous and wasteful, but I spend on my needs and desires and things that give me pleasure. I know that my subconscious will provide all that I need from the Divine Source as I need it. As I give out money, I am telling my subconscious that there is plenty, and in doing so, my subconscious will return with plenty tenfold. I will not hoard or worry that there is not enough to go around or that I cannot afford something because in doing so I am sending the wrong message and attracting more of "not enough to go around." I trust in the Divine Source to provide for me, and I show my faith by spending without guilt or fear. All the cash that I need or ask for is instantly manifested. I see my bank accounts filling up and money coming to me from all kinds of sources in unexpected ways. I now circulate this money, and as I give with faith, I will receive more.

Take a moment to reflect and meditate on this paragraph, asking what it means to you. Write down any insights that you have or reword it into what is meaningful to you.

DAY 25

Commit to Giving to Others

Remember to do "Getting into the Zone" before you start.

Stand in your Power Position. While holding and rubbing your pendant, read the following paragraph out loud:

I commit part of my income to helping others. I give without regret, without conditions, and without expectation. I send with this financial contribution a desire to raise the consciousness level of the receiver, so that they may ask for abundance from the Divine Source themselves. As I give generously, I am impressing upon my subconscious my abundance and my desire to have money to give. My subconscious will return to me tenfold what I have given. I will, in addition, give freely of my time and give freely of my love to others. My subconscious will return to me an abundance of time and love. Therefore today I give freely my money, my time, and my love. I expect nothing in return, and I gladly receive and say thanks as I am returned the same from the Divine Source.

Take a moment to reflect and meditate on this paragraph, asking what it means to you. Write down any insights that you have or reword it into what is meaningful to you.

DAY 26

I Am Part of a Team

Remember to do "Getting into the Zone" before you start.

Stand in your Power Position. While holding and rubbing your pendant, read the following paragraph out loud:

Before I was incarnated into this life, I made an agreement for my life's purpose. I left my friends in spirit within the Divine Source Energy, and these spirits agreed to be my guides and help me through life. When I connect through my subconscious to the Divine Source Energy, I am also connecting with these spirit guide helpers. When I feel joy, my spirit guides feel physical joy through me. Therefore, it is my life's purpose to feel joy, not just for myself but for my team. It is part of my commitment to my team to live an abundant life in financial freedom so that they may experience joy through me. Money flows freely to me, and I use this money for what gives me happiness. I use this money to afford the experiences that bring me happiness. As I bring myself joy, I bring this joy to others.

Take a moment to reflect and meditate on this paragraph, asking what it means to you. Write down any insights that you have or reword it into what is meaningful to you.

DAY 27

I Vow to Set My Comfort Level Higher

DAY 27

Remember to do "Getting into the Zone" before you start.

Stand in your Power Position. While holding and rubbing your pendant, read the following paragraph out loud:

> *I now know that I am the creator of all things, relationships, and experiences that come into my life through my subconscious and my connection to the Divine Source. I now know that the only limit of such creations is my imagination. I make a commitment to get out of my comfort zone and to create greater abundance, greater freedom, and greater accomplishments in my life. I do this not only for me, but for my team and for the benefit of everyone as a whole. I make a commitment to set my goals higher, to experience higher financial abundance, and to live in accordance with the greatness that was designed for me. I now ask to be showered with financial abundance. I trust that my bank accounts will be overflowing. I trust that I will have an abundance of money for all my desires and an excess to give to others.*

Take a moment to reflect and meditate on this paragraph, asking what it means to you. Write down any insights that you have or reword it into what is meaningful to you.

DAY 28

I Follow the Insights I Have Been Given

Remember to do "Getting into the Zone" before you start.

Stand in your Power Position. While holding and rubbing your pendant, read the following paragraph out loud:

I am now communicating clearly with my subconscious. Everything my conscious mind desires, my subconscious brings to me, immediately and in the perfect way. My subconscious brings me the gift of insight so that I may decipher my desires and follow my Life's Plan. I am aware of these knowings and I follow my instincts, as this is the way my subconscious directs me. I ask my subconscious to direct my thoughts to the path of prosperity so that I may think thoughts that bring me happiness and financial abundance in the most perfect ways. I ask that my subconscious bring me an abundance of money and increase my cash flow many times over. I ask that I am aware of the insights to receive this cash and that I am aware of the insights that direct me to the physical means through which this cash will be delivered.

Take a moment to reflect and meditate on this paragraph, asking what it means to you. Write down any insights that you have or reword it into what is meaningful to you.

DAY 29

I Live in Abundance

Remember to do "Getting into the Zone" before you start.

Stand in your Power Position. While holding and rubbing your pendant, read the following paragraph out loud:

I now live my life in abundance. I continually attract wealth and prosperity. My cups are all overflowing. My bank accounts are full, and money comes to me in unexpected ways. I am blessed with success and fulfillment in my career. I am awarded with financial abundance in all aspects of my life. I easily and happily pay all my expenses each month with plenty left over. I shower others with my generosity—I give to family, friends, and strangers. Everything I desire is now manifesting in my life. There is nothing that I cannot have or do. All experiences that I wish to have are now manifesting in my life. I live in complete financial freedom, having the choice to spend my days as I desire. I no longer suffer lack. I do not speak of lack and it does not exist in my experience. I have complete trust in my subconscious and it works perfectly, delivering from the Divine Source whatever I desire.

Take a moment to reflect and meditate on this paragraph, asking what it means to you. Write down any insights that you have or reword it into what is meaningful to you.

_____

_____

_____

_____

_____

_____

_____

_____

_____

_____

DAY 30

My Subconscious Is Now Programmed

DAY 30

Remember to do "Getting into the Zone" before you start.

Stand in your Power Position. While holding and rubbing your pendant, read the following paragraph out loud:

My subconscious works automatically, always and perfectly, bringing me all that I ask for or focus on. My subconscious is now programmed to bring me wealth, health, and prosperity. My subconscious is now programmed to bring me all that I desire to experience and all that brings me happiness and joy. My subconscious is programmed to bring me financial abundance, in the highest of goodness. My subconscious overflows my bank accounts and brings success to all that I touch. I shall worry no more, as my connection to the Divine Source is unbreakable and my subconscious works perfectly, every day, in every way.

Now, as you hold and rub your pendant, go back to the beginning. Starting at Day 1, read each day's *italicized* paragraph out loud, including the one above (Day 30).

You may add any insights or notes to yourself from the entire 30-day program.

THE REST OF YOUR LIFE

Is financial abundance flowing more easily? Are you allowing more joy and happiness in your life? Are you finding that you can better afford the pleasures in life? Have you improved your income streams? Do you have a new outlook on life?

This program is meant to set your subconscious in the right direction, but you need to keep reminding your conscious mind how to communicate with your subconscious. Continue to ask for and focus on only the things that you want to manifest. This course was designed to set you on your Divine Life Path, but it is your job to continue this new way of being.

Periodically reread these exercises and repeat the whole 30-day course when you feel you are stepping off your path and need a refresher. For a speed refresher, you can run your pendant over the Table of Contents for Section II and ask that your pendant reconnect your subconscious to each of the daily exercises. Your pendant is already programmed, and just pointing it at the Table of Contents is sufficient. Alternatively, you can simply read the Table of Contents and your conscious mind will connect to your subconscious in the same way. Your subconscious is already programmed, and so just a pointer in the right direction will bring back all the programming you have already installed.

At this point, you may discard your pendant or you may continue to wear it as jewelry. Do not become superstitious about this object, thinking that your abundance somehow depends on it. It does not! This object was simply a connector to your subconscious, but you have programmed your subconscious to connect to your mind and you can now do it on your own.

FEEDBACK
Give your comments! Tell me your success story!

I would love to hear your personal experiences with this 30-day workshop. Please write and let me know what kind of overall results you received, as well as anything that particularly resonated with you. I am very interested to know your story and how this workbook may have helped you, especially any unique ways your desires are brought to you and if there were any parts that were difficult for you. I may use your feedback on my website or in other media so, in writing to me, you are giving your permission to use your story and comments, unless you also include a note in your correspondence that you do not want it published. I cannot promise to respond personally to all your emails but I do review my own email. I look forward to hearing from you!

Gail Thackray

Please email me at:
feedback@30daystoprosperitybook.com

To learn more about Gail's speaking engagements, books, television series, workshops and live events, please visit her website:
www.GailThackray.com

MONEY-BACK GUARANTEE

I am so confident that you will see marked results after following this program that I am investing in your success by offering you a money-back guarantee if this program does not work for you.

Only you know if you have really given your all to this program. It only works if you give it your full attention and follow each step with dedication. If you are not experiencing the results that you had hoped for, first take a close look at your commitment. Have you been sabotaging your results by sending opposing messages to your subconscious? Have you been asking out loud for abundance but in the back of your mind thinking, "This will never work"? Are you asking for something and then sending messages of disappointment because you don't have it yet and therefore sending your subconscious more of the "I don't have it yet" experience? You owe it to yourself to give this a real, honest commitment.

If after all this, you feel you have really gained nothing from this book, I will happily refund your purchase price. However, be sure that you are not asking for a refund before honestly putting forth your full effort, or are asking for a refund for the wrong reasons.

If you are still not satisfied with your results, send your copy of this book along with your receipt to Indian Springs Publishing, P.O. Box 286, La Cañada, California 91012. Please enclose a stamped, self-addressed envelope marked with the name and address of where you want your refund to be sent. For the refund, you need to have followed this program and done all the exercises as prescribed. **All of the spaces in the book for your insights should be filled in, in order for you to receive your refund. If you made additional notes, please submit those as well.** The refund is limited to the actual purchase price of the book (excluding shipping and handling).

CPSIA information can be obtained at www.ICGtesting.com
Printed in the USA
BVOW022352230413

318967BV00002B/3/P

9 780984 844005